The Countryside

in pictures

Pictures
to share

For Keith

**Pictures
to share**

First published in 2006 by
Pictures to Share Community Interest Company,
a UK based social enterprise that publishes
illustrated books for older people.

www.picturestoshare.co.uk

ISBN 10: 0-9553940-1-5
ISBN 13: 978-0-9553940-1-0

Front Cover: Encounter on the Way to the Field 1897
        by Thomas Ludwig Herbst (1845-1915)
        The Bridgeman Art Library/Getty Images
Endpapers: Butterflies © Ann Bridges www.ann-bridges.com
Title page: Berry Garland by Jan Kerton.
        From A-Z of Stumpwork/Country Bumkin Publications,
        Australia www.countrybumkin.com.au
Back cover: Detail from Fidelity by Briton Riviere (1840-1920)
        Lady Lever Gallery, National Museums, Liverpool
        Detail from Boy with rabbits © M.E.R.L. Reading
        Detail from Hare © Mike Roberts

The Countryside

in pictures

Edited by Helen J Bate

What a
glorious morning
is this.

Quotation: Samuel Adams (1722-1803)
Painting: Cockerel © Mary Ann Rogers www.marogers.com

Come we to the summer,

to the summer we will come,

For the woods are full of bluebells
and the hedges full of bloom,

And the crow is on the oak
a-building of her nest,

And love is burning diamonds
in my true lover's breast;

Quotation from 'Summer' by John Clare (1793-1864)
Main photograph: English beech forest by Rosemary Calvert.
The Image Bank/Getty Images
Small photograph: Bluebell by Nigel Downer. Taxi/Getty Images

Stolen sweets are always sweeter;

Stolen kisses much completer;
Stolen looks are nice in chapels,
Stolen, stolen, be your apples.

Quotation from 'Songs of Fairies Robbing an Orchard'
1830 by James Henry Leigh Hunt (1784-1859)
Main photograph: Fruit Pickers by Reg Speller. Hulton Archive/Getty Images
Small photograph: Apple core © John Farrow

If you can catch a hare

and look into its eye
you will see the whole world.

Quotation from 'A Calendar of Hares' by Anna Crowe
From A Secret History of Rhubarb, published by Mariscat Press, Glasgow
Photographs: Hare © Mike Roberts

I meant to do my work today

But a brown bird sang in the apple tree,
And a butterfly flitted across a field,
And all the leaves were calling me.

And the wind went sighing over the land
Tossing the grasses to and fro,
And a rainbow held out its shining hand
So what could I do but laugh and go?

Quotation from 'I Meant to Do My Work Today' by Richard LeGallienne.
Reprinted by permission of The Society of Authors/Estate of Richard LeGallienne
Photograph by Grant Dixon. Lonely Planet Images/Getty Images

I will hold my house in the high wood

Within a walk of the sea,
And the men that were boys
when I was a boy
Shall sit and drink with me.

Quotation: from 'The South Country' from Complete Verse by Hilaire Belloc (1870-1953)
© The Estate of Hilaire Belloc 1970 reproduced by permission of PFD (www.pfd.co.uk)
on behalf of the Estate of Hilaire Belloc.
Photographs: Boy with dead rabbits. Photographer unknown.
Museum of English Rural Life, The University of Reading. www.reading.ac.uk/Instits/im/

Country wedding

As the newly married pair left the church to the strains of the wedding march and the pealing of the church bells, they passed beneath a magnificent archway, formed by the wands of schoolgirls. There was a large crowd of well-wishers, and led by the village schoolboys who were lined up on the green, they cheered heartily.

On leaving the church, the youngest scholar, Dorothy Hopley, gracefully strewed the path to the road with yellow flowers.

Wedding gifts included a pearl and diamond pendant from the estate tenants, and a silver tea caddy from the indoor and outdoor servants at Bolesworth Castle.

Quotation: Newspaper cutting reporting the wedding of Eleanor Barbour at Harthill Church, Cheshire, 1910
Painting: A Country Wedding by Judy Joel.
The Bridgeman Art Library/Getty Images

Creep into thy narrow bed,

Creep, and let no more be said!

Let the long contention cease!
Geese are swans, and swans
are geese.

Let them have it how they will!
Thou art tired; best be still.

Quotation from 'The Last Word' 1867
by Matthew Arnold (1822-1888)
Photographs: Details from Mute swans on River Tweed
by Laurie Campbell. Stone/Getty Images

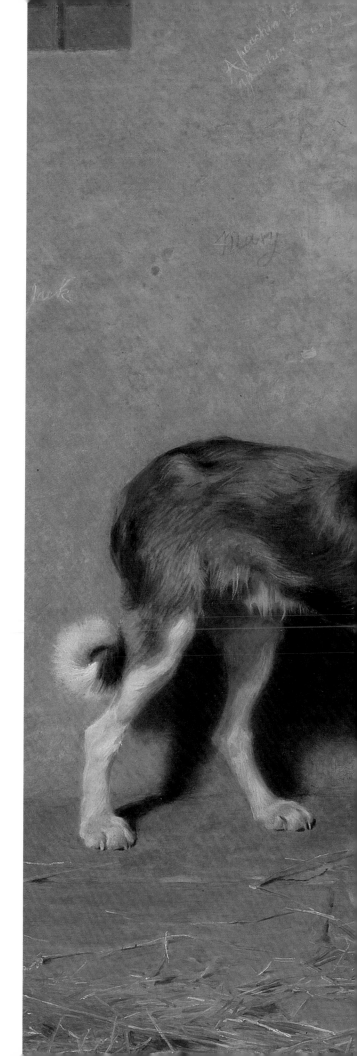

Country road

Like the main-travelled
road of life, it is traversed
by many classes of people,
but the poor and the
weary predominate.

Quotation from Main Travelled Roads 1891,
by Hamlin Garland (1860-1940)
Painting: Fidelity by Briton Riviere (1840-1920)
Lady Lever Gallery, National Museums Liverpool

Everyone has a talent at twenty-five.

The difficult thing is
to have it at fifty.

Quotation: Edgar Degas (1834-1917)
Photographs: Riding instructor by Reg Speller.
Hulton Archive/Getty Images

Heavy Horse

Andy Scott's 15ft high
galvanised steel sculpture
of a Clydesdale horse stands
by the M8 in Glasgow.

See more of Andy Scott's work at www.aqza25.dsl.pipex.com/andy
Photographs © James McKillop

A bird in the hand

is worth two in the bush.

Quotation: Traditional saying
Main photograph: Christmas Is Coming by William Vanderson.
Hulton Archive/Getty Images

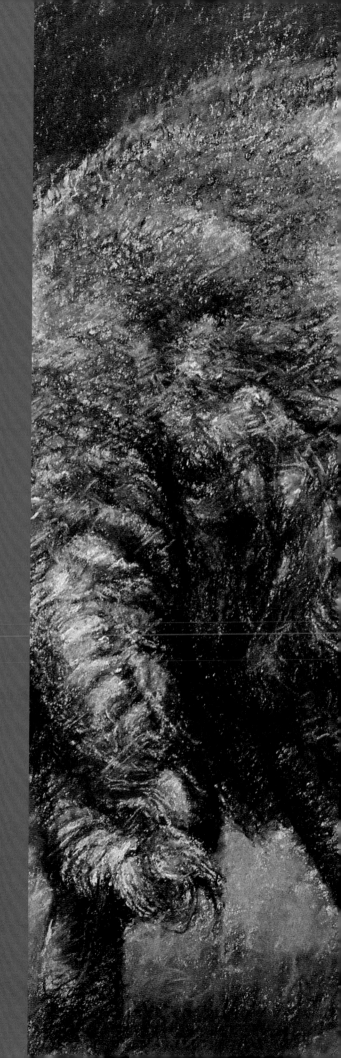

A flock of sheep that leisurely pass by,

One after one;
the sound of rain and bees

Murmuring; the fall of rivers,
winds and seas,

Smooth fields, white sheets
of water, and pure sky;

I've thought of all by turns,
and still I lie

Sleepless.

Quotation from 'To Sleep'
by William Wordsworth (1770-1850)
Pastel painting: 'The First Suckle'
© 1991 Keith Bowen from 'Snowdon Shepherd'
Published by Pavilion Books Ltd, London.

The woods are lovely, dark and deep.

But I have promises to keep,
And miles to go before I sleep.
And miles to go before I sleep.

Quotation from 'Stopping by Woods on a Snowy Evening'
by Robert Frost (1875-1963)
Main photograph: Sunbeams in Forest © iStockphoto.com/AVTG.
Small photograph: Mouse © Steve McWilliam (rECOrd. Chester)

**Pictures
to share**

Acknowledgements

Our thanks to the many contributors who have allowed their
text or imagery to be used for a reduced or no fee.
Thanks also to all those who assisted in the development of this
book by helping with or taking part in trials; especially Sally Reid,
Occupational Therapist, of Prospect House Nursing Home,
Malpas, and John Thompson, Activities Co-ordinator
at Crawfords Walk Nursing Home, Chester.

All effort has been made to contact copyright holders.
If you own the copyright for work that is represented, but have
not been contacted, please get in touch via our website.

Thanks to our sponsors

The UnLtd Millennium Awards Scheme
The LankellyChase Foundation
The Rayne Foundation
The Cheshire Partnership
Cheshire and Warrington Social Enterprise Partnership

Some quotations have been provided by
'Chambers Dictionary of Quotations',
Chambers Harrap Publishers Ltd, 2005

Published by

Pictures to Share Community Interest Company.
Peckforton, Cheshire
www.picturestoshare.co.uk

Printed in England by
Burlington Press, 1 Station Road, Foxton CB22 6SA